Mozambique

Travel Guide

Your Ultimate Companion to Discover the Rich Culture, Pristine Beaches and Vibrant Wildlife of Mozambique

Tyler Rivers

Disclaimer

The pictures featured in this book are for artistic purposes only and do not necessarily represent the actual locations referenced in the text. While every effort has been made to ensure the accuracy of the information contained in this guide, neither the author nor the publisher assumes any responsibility for errors or omissions, or for any consequences arising from the use of the information contained herein.

Table of Content

Introduction

In this book, we will take you on an exciting journey through the captivating landscapes, vibrant culture, and rich history of Mozambique. Whether you're an adventurous traveler, a wildlife enthusiast, a beach lover, or simply curious about exploring new destinations, this guide has something for everyone.

Mozambique, located on the southeastern coast of Africa, offers a unique blend of stunning natural beauty, diverse wildlife, and a fascinating fusion of African, Portuguese, and Arab influences. With its pristine beaches, tropical islands, lush national parks, and bustling cities, Mozambique promises an unforgettable travel experience.

In the following chapters, we will delve into the different aspects of this enchanting country. From the bustling capital city of Maputo to the remote islands in the Indian Ocean, we will provide you with in-depth information to help you plan your perfect itinerary. You'll discover the best places to visit, where to find the most breathtaking beaches, the top wildlife reserves to explore, and the hidden gems that will make your journey truly special.

We'll also take a closer look at Mozambique's rich history, from its colonial past to its struggle for independence and its emergence as a thriving African nation. By understanding the cultural context of the country, you'll gain a deeper appreciation for its traditions, art, and architecture.

Moreover, this guide will provide practical advice on how to make the most of your trip to Mozambique. We'll cover topics such as transportation options, visa requirements, health and safety tips, and recommended travel seasons. Additionally, we'll emphasize the importance of responsible tourism and how you can contribute to the preservation of Mozambique's natural and cultural heritage.

So, whether you're planning a relaxing beach holiday, an exciting safari adventure, or a cultural exploration, Mozambique Travel Guide will serve as your indispensable companion. Get ready to immerse yourself in the warmth of Mozambican hospitality, indulge in mouthwatering cuisine, and create memories that will last a lifetime.

CHAPTER 1

INTRODUCTION TO MOZAMBIQUE

Welcome to the captivating world of Mozambique, a country brimming with natural wonders, vibrant culture, and a rich history waiting to be explored. Nestled along the southeastern coast of Africa, Mozambique is a hidden gem that offers a unique and unforgettable travel experience. In this chapter, we will embark on a journey to uncover the essence of this enchanting nation, from its geography and climate to its diverse heritage and attractions.

Geography: A Land of Diversity

Stretching over 2,500 kilometers (1,500 miles) along the Indian Ocean, Mozambique boasts a diverse and awe-inspiring landscape. The country is bordered by six countries, including Tanzania to the north, Malawi and Zambia to the northwest, Zimbabwe to the west, Eswatini (formerly Swaziland) to the southwest, and South Africa to the south.

The Mozambican mainland is characterized by vast plains, rolling hills, and majestic mountains. The Great Rift Valley, an ancient geological formation, traverses the western part of the country, offering breathtaking vistas and fertile lands.

To the east, the coastline is a tapestry of sandy beaches, palm-fringed islands, and vibrant coral reefs. The archipelagos of Bazaruto and Quirimbas, among others, are home to some of the most pristine and idyllic islands in the Indian Ocean.

Mozambique's geographical diversity extends inland to its national parks and wildlife reserves. The Gorongosa National Park, located in the central region, is a biodiversity hotspot renowned for its diverse ecosystems and remarkable wildlife. From elephants and lions to zebras and buffalo, the park offers thrilling game viewing opportunities.

Climate: Sunshine and Tropical Breezes

Mozambique experiences a tropical climate, making it an ideal destination for those seeking warmth and sunshine. The country has two primary seasons: the dry season, which lasts from April to September, and the wet season, which occurs from October to March.

During the dry season, temperatures range from 25°C to 35°C (77°F to 95°F), with low humidity and minimal rainfall. This period is perfect for beach lovers and water sports enthusiasts, as the clear skies and calm waters offer an ideal setting for relaxation and adventure.

The wet season brings refreshing rains that rejuvenate the landscape and support Mozambique's lush vegetation. While the humidity rises, temperatures remain pleasant, ranging from 25°C to 30°C (77°F to 86°F). The rain showers, although sporadic, create a vibrant atmosphere and add an extra dimension to the country's natural beauty.

Cultural Melting Pot: A Tapestry of Traditions

Mozambique's rich cultural heritage is a tapestry woven from a blend of African, Portuguese, and Arab influences. The country's history and diverse ethnic groups have shaped its unique identity, creating a cultural mosaic that is both fascinating and welcoming.

The Bantu peoples, including the Makhuwa, Tsonga, and Shona, form the majority of Mozambique's population. Their traditions, languages, and vibrant customs reflect the ancestral roots of the nation. The Makonde people, renowned for their intricate wood carvings, have contributed significantly to Mozambique's artistic legacy.

The influence of Portuguese colonization, which lasted for nearly five centuries, is evident in Mozambique's language, architecture, and cuisine.

Portuguese is the official language of the country, and the colonial-era buildings in cities like Maputo showcase an eclectic blend of European and African architectural styles.

The Arab heritage, dating back to the ancient trading routes along the coast, has left an indelible mark on Mozambique's cultural tapestry. The Swahili language, influenced by Arabic, is spoken in the northern coastal regions, while the coastal cities bear testimony to the rich history of Arab traders.

Exploring Mozambique's History

To truly understand Mozambique and its people, it is essential to delve into the country's historical journey. From ancient civilizations to colonial rule and the fight for independence, Mozambique's past has shaped its present and offers valuable insights into its cultural fabric.

Archaeological evidence suggests that Mozambique's coastal regions were inhabited as early as the 1st century AD. The Kingdom of Mapungubwe, which thrived between the 9th and 13th centuries, traded gold and ivory with the Arab merchants, leaving traces of a prosperous civilization.

In the 15th century, Portuguese explorers, including Vasco da Gama, arrived on the shores of Mozambique, marking the beginning of European influence in the region. The

Portuguese established trading posts and later colonized Mozambique, exploiting its resources and introducing Christianity and their language.

The struggle for independence from Portuguese rule intensified in the mid-20th century, culminating in Mozambique's independence on June 25, 1975. The country faced numerous challenges in the post-independence era, including a civil war that lasted from 1977 to 1992. However, Mozambique emerged from this turbulent period with resilience and determination, embarking on a path of progress and development.

Attractions and Experiences: Mozambique Unveiled

Mozambique's allure lies in its diverse range of attractions and experiences. From vibrant cities to pristine beaches, from wildlife encounters to cultural immersion, there is something for every traveler in this captivating country.

The capital city, Maputo, is a vibrant metropolis that blends the old and the new. Explore its colonial architecture, visit the bustling markets, and indulge in the city's vibrant music and dance scene. Sample the delicious flavors of Mozambican cuisine, known for its fusion of African, Portuguese, and Indian influences.

For beach enthusiasts, Mozambique offers a coastal paradise like no other. From the turquoise waters of the Bazaruto Archipelago to the remote and untouched Quirimbas Islands, there are endless opportunities for relaxation, water sports, and island hopping adventures. Snorkel or dive among vibrant coral reefs teeming with marine life, or simply bask in the sun on the powdery white sands.

Nature lovers will be captivated by Mozambique's national parks and wildlife reserves. Embark on a safari in the Gorongosa National Park, where you can witness the incredible biodiversity and participate in conservation efforts. Discover the Niassa Reserve, one of Africa's largest protected areas, home to elephants, lions, and the elusive African wild dog.

Immerse yourself in Mozambique's vibrant culture by visiting local villages, participating in traditional ceremonies, and witnessing traditional dance and music performances. Learn about the art of wood carving, explore local markets, and engage with the warm and welcoming Mozambican people.

In the upcoming chapters, we will delve deeper into Mozambique's treasures, providing you with detailed information on each region, its attractions, activities, and practical travel tips. So, get ready to embark on a remarkable adventure as we unlock the secrets of Mozambique, a country that will undoubtedly capture your heart and leave you with unforgettable memories.

CHAPTER 2

UNRAVELING MOZAMBIQUE'S HISTORY AND CULTURE

As you embark on your journey through Mozambique, it is essential to understand the country's rich history and vibrant culture. Mozambique's past is a tapestry woven with diverse influences, shaped by the interactions of indigenous peoples, Arab traders, and Portuguese colonizers. This chapter will take you on a captivating exploration of Mozambique's historical roots and the cultural mosaic that thrives within its borders.

1. **Ancient Origins**: Mozambique's history dates back thousands of years, with evidence of human habitation in the region since the Paleolithic era. The Bantu migration from West Africa brought new agricultural practices and linguistic diversity to the area. Ancient trade routes connected Mozambique to distant lands, fostering cultural exchange and the growth of thriving coastal settlements.

2. **Arab Influence**: From the 7th century onwards, Arab traders ventured to the shores of Mozambique, establishing trading posts along the coast. The Swahili culture, influenced by Arab and Bantu traditions,

flourished in cities like Sofala and Kilwa. The Arab merchants introduced new crops, such as rice and coconuts, and brought Islam, which remains an integral part of Mozambique's cultural fabric.

3. **Portuguese Colonial Era**: In the late 15th century, Portuguese explorer Vasco da Gama arrived in Mozambique, marking the beginning of Portuguese colonization. The Portuguese established a series of trading forts, exploiting the region's resources, including gold, ivory, and slaves. Mozambique became an integral part of the Portuguese Empire and played a significant role in the transatlantic slave trade.

4. **Struggle for Independence**: Mozambique's journey to independence was marked by years of resistance against Portuguese colonial rule. The Mozambique Liberation Front (FRELIMO) emerged as a prominent liberation movement, advocating for self-determination and the end of colonial oppression. After a protracted armed struggle, Mozambique finally gained independence on June 25, 1975, becoming a sovereign nation.

5. **Post-Independence Challenges**: The post-independence era brought its own set of challenges for

Mozambique. The country faced a devastating civil war that lasted from 1977 to 1992, leaving a trail of destruction and economic hardship. However, Mozambique managed to rebuild and transition into a stable democracy, fostering national reconciliation and promoting economic development.

6. **Cultural Diversity**: Mozambique is a cultural melting pot, home to over 40 ethnic groups, each with its distinct traditions, languages, and art forms. The Makonde people, known for their intricate wood carvings, the Chopi people with their enchanting music and dance, and the Tsonga people with their vibrant textiles are just a few examples of the cultural diversity found in the country.

7. **Music and Dance**: Music and dance are integral parts of Mozambican culture, reflecting the country's historical and cultural influences. Traditional music styles like marrabenta and marrabenta star emerged, blending African rhythms with Portuguese guitar melodies. The energetic and rhythmic dances, such as the Mapiko dance performed by the Makonde people, showcase Mozambique's vibrant spirit.

8. **Cuisine**: Mozambican cuisine is a delightful fusion of African, Portuguese, and Indian flavors. The staple food is maize, which is often enjoyed in the form of xima, a thick porridge. Seafood, including prawns, calamari, and fish, is abundant along the coast and features prominently in coastal cuisine. The use of spices like piri-piri adds a fiery kick to many dishes, while cashews and tropical fruits add a touch of sweetness.

9. **Art and Handicrafts**: Mozambique's artistic heritage is diverse and captivating. Skilled artisans create intricate wood carvings, pottery, and woven baskets, often depicting scenes from daily life or mythical creatures. The vibrant Capulana fabric, with its bold patterns and colors, is widely used for clothing and home decor. Exploring local markets and craft centers allows visitors to appreciate the talent and craftsmanship of Mozambique's artisans.

10. **Festivals and Celebrations**: Mozambique's festivals and celebrations are vibrant and joyous occasions that showcase the country's cultural richness. The Marrabenta Festival in Maputo celebrates the country's musical heritage, while the Timbila Festival in Zavala highlights traditional Chopi

music and dance. The Mapiko Mask Festival, held in several communities, features masked performances with deep spiritual and cultural significance.

Immersing yourself in Mozambique's history and culture will enhance your travel experience and deepen your connection with the country and its people. From exploring ancient ruins to engaging with local communities, Mozambique offers a captivating tapestry of traditions, music, cuisine, and artistic expressions that will leave a lasting impression on your journey.

CHAPTER 3

PLANNING YOUR ADVENTURE IN MOZAMBIQUE

As you embark on your journey to Mozambique, proper planning is essential to ensure a smooth and enjoyable adventure. From deciding when to go and how to get there, to understanding entry requirements and creating an itinerary, this chapter will guide you through the necessary steps for planning your trip to this captivating country.

Choosing the Best Time to Visit

Mozambique's climate is characterized by two distinct seasons: the dry season and the wet season. The dry season, which runs from May to October, is generally considered the best time to visit as the weather is sunny, warm, and ideal for outdoor activities. The wet season, from November to April, brings occasional heavy rains and higher humidity, but it also presents a unique opportunity to witness Mozambique's lush landscapes in full bloom.

The specific time of your visit may also depend on your interests. If you're a wildlife enthusiast, consider planning your trip during the dry season when animals congregate around water sources, making them easier to spot during safaris. If diving or snorkeling is on your itinerary, aim for the wet season when the water visibility is at its best.

Entry Requirements and Visa Information

Before traveling to Mozambique, it's important to familiarize yourself with the entry requirements. Most visitors will need a valid passport with at least six months of validity remaining. Depending on your nationality, you may require a visa to enter the country.

To obtain a tourist visa, you can apply in advance at a Mozambican embassy or consulate in your home country. Alternatively, some nationalities are eligible for visa-on-arrival, allowing you to obtain a visa upon arrival at major airports and border crossings. It is advisable to check the most up-to-date visa regulations before your trip to ensure a hassle-free entry.

Getting There and Transportation Options

Reaching Mozambique is relatively straightforward, with several international airports serving the country. The main entry point is Maputo International Airport, which receives flights from various African and international destinations.

Other airports, such as Vilankulo and Pemba, offer convenient access to specific regions of Mozambique.

Once you arrive in Mozambique, various transportation options are available to explore the country. Domestic flights are a popular choice for covering long distances, especially if you're short on time. LAM Mozambique Airlines and other regional carriers operate scheduled flights between major cities and tourist hubs.

For a more immersive experience, consider traveling by road. Mozambique has a well-connected road network, although conditions may vary, especially in rural areas. Renting a car or hiring a private driver allows you to explore at your own pace and discover hidden gems along the way.

Creating Your Itinerary

Mozambique offers a diverse range of attractions, from stunning beaches and vibrant cities to wildlife-rich national parks and cultural sites. When creating your itinerary, consider your interests, available time, and preferred activities.

Start by exploring the capital city, Maputo, where you can soak in the lively atmosphere, visit historical landmarks like the Fortress of Maputo, and indulge in local cuisine at the bustling Central Market. From Maputo, venture to the southern coastline, known for its palm-fringed beaches and excellent diving opportunities. The Bazaruto Archipelago, a collection of picturesque islands, is a must-visit destination for beach lovers and water sports enthusiasts.

In the north, the Quirimbas Archipelago beckons with its pristine beaches and luxury resorts. Combine your beach stay with a visit to the Quirimbas National Park, home to diverse marine life and lush mangrove forests.

For a wildlife safari, head to Gorongosa National Park or Niassa Reserve, where you can spot elephants, lions, and an array of bird species. These protected areas offer a chance to connect with nature and contribute to conservation efforts.

As you plan your itinerary, allow for flexibility and ample time to relax and immerse yourself in the local culture. Mozambique's relaxed pace of life invites you to slow down, savor each moment, and embrace the warmth of its people.

Accommodation Options

Mozambique boasts a wide range of accommodation options to suit every budget and preference. In major cities like Maputo and Beira, you'll find luxury hotels, boutique guesthouses, and international chains. Along the coastline, beachfront resorts and eco-lodges offer idyllic settings for a tranquil getaway.

For a more immersive experience, consider staying in locally owned lodges and guesthouses, especially in rural areas. These establishments often provide unique insights into Mozambican culture and contribute directly to the local economy.

It's advisable to book accommodations in advance, particularly during the peak season, to secure your preferred choice and ensure a seamless travel experience.

CHAPTER 4

EXPLORING THE COASTAL GEMS: BEACHES AND ISLANDS

When it comes to breathtaking coastal landscapes, Mozambique truly stands out. With its pristine beaches, crystal-clear waters, and idyllic islands, this country offers a tropical paradise for beach lovers and sun seekers. In Chapter 4, we will embark on a journey to explore the coastal gems of Mozambique, discovering the hidden treasures that await you along its stunning shoreline.

Maputo Beaches

Our exploration begins in the vibrant capital city of Maputo, where you'll find a variety of beautiful beaches just a stone's throw away. Maputo Beach, also known as Ponta d'Ouro, is a popular destination for both locals and tourists. With its golden sands and azure waters, it's the perfect spot for swimming, sunbathing, and beachside relaxation. If you're feeling adventurous, you can even try your hand at surfing or join a diving excursion to explore the colorful marine life beneath the surface.

Bazaruto Archipelago

From Maputo, we venture north to one of Mozambique's most renowned coastal destinations – the Bazaruto Archipelago. Comprised of five main islands – Bazaruto, Benguerra, Magaruque, Santa Carolina, and Bangue – this archipelago is a true tropical paradise. Here, you'll find pristine beaches, swaying palm trees, and luxury resorts that cater to your every need. Whether you choose to relax on the white sands, snorkel in the crystal-clear waters, or embark on a sailing adventure, the Bazaruto Archipelago offers a slice of paradise that will leave you in awe.

Quirimbas Archipelago:

Continuing our journey up the coast, we arrive at another coastal gem – the Quirimbas Archipelago. This group of islands, stretching along the northern coast of Mozambique, is a haven for nature enthusiasts and those seeking a remote island getaway. The Quirimbas Archipelago boasts a rich marine ecosystem, making it a prime destination for diving and snorkeling. As you explore the underwater world, you'll encounter vibrant coral reefs, playful dolphins, and a myriad of colorful fish.

Don't miss the opportunity to visit Ibo Island, with its fascinating blend of historical ruins and local culture, offering a glimpse into Mozambique's past.

Tofo Beach

Located in the Inhambane Province, Tofo Beach is renowned for its incredible marine biodiversity, particularly its encounters with whale sharks and manta rays. As you stroll along the beach, you'll be captivated by the picturesque scenery and the laid-back atmosphere. Diving enthusiasts will find themselves in paradise, as Tofo Beach offers world-class diving opportunities to explore the vibrant coral reefs and encounter majestic marine creatures up close. If you prefer to stay dry, you can still enjoy the beauty of the ocean by taking a boat trip or going on a thrilling dhow cruise.

Pemba

Our coastal exploration wouldn't be complete without a visit to Pemba, the capital of the Cabo Delgado Province. Pemba is known for its stunning beaches, charming fishing villages, and a bustling harbor. Wimbe Beach, in particular, attracts visitors with its palm-fringed shores and calm waters.

Here, you can indulge in water sports such as snorkeling, kayaking, and windsurfing. After a day of seaside adventures, don't forget to savor the delicious seafood delicacies that Pemba has to offer.

CHAPTER 5

THE COASTAL GEMS: BEACHES AND ISLANDS

As the sun rises over the azure waters of the Indian Ocean, Mozambique reveals its coastal gems, beckoning travelers to explore its breathtaking beaches and enchanting islands. In this chapter, we will delve into the coastal wonders that make Mozambique a paradise for beach lovers and water enthusiasts.

The Magic of the Quirimbas Archipelago

Nestled off the northern coast of Mozambique, the Quirimbas Archipelago is a collection of 32 coral islands, each with its own unique charm. These pristine islands, surrounded by vibrant coral reefs, offer a haven of tranquility and natural beauty. From the largest island of Ibo, with its rich historical heritage, to the remote and untouched islands of Quilalea and Medjumbe, the Quirimbas Archipelago is a paradise waiting to be explored.

Bazaruto Archipelago: A Tropical Paradise

Moving south along the coast, we arrive at the Bazaruto Archipelago, a group of islands renowned for their untouched beauty and abundant marine life.

The main islands of Bazaruto, Benguerra, and Magaruque are surrounded by turquoise waters, vibrant coral reefs, and pristine white sand beaches. Snorkelers and divers will be in awe of the diverse marine ecosystem, where they can swim alongside manta rays, turtles, and colorful tropical fish.

Tofo Beach: A Surfer's Paradise

For those seeking a mix of relaxation and adventure, Tofo Beach is a must-visit destination. Located on the southern coast of Mozambique, Tofo Beach is a haven for surfers, offering perfect waves and a vibrant surf culture. Even if you're not a surfer, the laid-back atmosphere, stunning sunsets, and warm hospitality of the locals will make you feel right at home.

Vilankulo: Gateway to the Archipelago

As the gateway to the Bazaruto Archipelago, Vilankulo is a charming coastal town that blends Mozambican culture with a touch of international flair. From here, you can embark on a boat trip to explore the nearby islands, go snorkeling or scuba diving in the marine park, or simply relax on the pristine beaches.

Don't miss the opportunity to savor freshly caught seafood at one of the local restaurants, where the flavors of Mozambique come alive.

Inhambane: A Cultural and Historical Hub

Further south along the coast lies the historic town of Inhambane, a place steeped in Mozambique's cultural and colonial heritage. Explore the narrow streets lined with colonial-era buildings, visit the local markets brimming with vibrant colors and flavors, and immerse yourself in the local way of life. From Inhambane, you can also venture to nearby beach towns like Tofo and Barra, where you can enjoy water activities, indulge in delicious seafood, and witness the annual migration of humpback whales.

Pemba: Gateway to the Quirimbas

If you're planning to explore the Quirimbas Archipelago, Pemba is your starting point. This lively coastal city offers a blend of African, Arab, and Portuguese influences, evident in its architecture, cuisine, and cultural traditions. Spend some time exploring Pemba's vibrant markets, where you can find local crafts, spices, and fresh produce.

From Pemba, you can catch a flight or take a boat to the islands of the Quirimbas Archipelago, embarking on an unforgettable island-hopping adventure.

Island-Hopping: Creating Your Own Escape

One of the greatest joys of Mozambique's coastal wonders is the opportunity to embark on an island-hopping adventure. With countless islands scattered along the coastline, you can create your own personalized escape, hopping from one idyllic paradise to another. Whether you choose to snorkel in crystal-clear waters, indulge in beach picnics on deserted shores, or simply relax under the shade of a palm tree, each island has its own unique charm and allure.

CHAPTER 6

WILDLIFE AND NATURE RESERVES IN MOZAMBIQUE

As you venture into the wild heart of Mozambique, prepare to be captivated by its diverse and awe-inspiring wildlife. From the rugged savannahs and dense forests to the pristine coastal waters, this chapter will introduce you to the country's remarkable nature reserves and the fascinating creatures that call them home.

Gorongosa National Park

Located in central Mozambique, Gorongosa National Park is a conservation success story. Once devastated by civil war, the park has made a remarkable recovery, thanks to dedicated conservation efforts. Today, it stands as a testament to the resilience of nature. Embark on a safari through the park's lush landscapes, where you'll have the opportunity to spot an array of wildlife, including elephants, lions, hippos, and buffalo. The park is also renowned for its rich birdlife, making it a paradise for birdwatchers.

Niassa Reserve

Prepare to be transported to a pristine wilderness as you set foot in the Niassa Reserve, Mozambique's largest protected area. This vast expanse of untamed beauty covers over 42,000 square kilometers (16,200 square miles) and is home to an incredible variety of wildlife. Traverse the reserve's diverse ecosystems, from miombo woodlands to riverine forests, and encounter magnificent species such as elephants, lions, leopards, and African wild dogs. The Niassa Reserve offers a truly immersive and authentic safari experience.

Bazaruto Archipelago National Park

Escape to a tropical paradise in the Bazaruto Archipelago National Park, a collection of islands off Mozambique's coast. This marine park encompasses five islands: Bazaruto, Benguerra, Magaruque, Santa Carolina, and Bangue. The crystal-clear waters teem with vibrant coral reefs and a kaleidoscope of marine life, including dolphins, turtles, and a myriad of colorful fish. Snorkel or dive among these underwater wonders, or simply relax on the idyllic beaches, soaking up the sun and listening to the gentle lapping of the waves.

Quirimbas National Park

Situated in the far north of Mozambique, the Quirimbas National Park is a hidden gem awaiting discovery.

This remote and untouched paradise encompasses both land and sea, with pristine beaches, mangrove forests, and rich coral reefs. Explore the park's diverse habitats, keeping an eye out for elusive wildlife such as crocodiles, antelopes, and the rare dugong. The Quirimbas Archipelago, a string of tropical islands within the park, offers a tranquil escape and a chance to witness nesting turtles and graceful humpback whales during their migration season.

Maputo Special Reserve

Located just a short drive from Mozambique's capital city, Maputo Special Reserve offers a unique opportunity to combine wildlife encounters with urban exploration. This coastal reserve encompasses a variety of ecosystems, including wetlands, grasslands, and mangrove forests. Embark on a game drive or a boat safari along the Maputo River, where you may spot hippos, crocodiles, and an array of bird species. The reserve is also home to the elusive and endangered Samango monkeys, making it a prime destination for primate enthusiasts.

Marromeu Game Reserve

Nestled along the Zambezi River, the Marromeu Game Reserve showcases the incredible biodiversity of Mozambique's wetlands. This expansive reserve is renowned for its large herds of elephants, as well as buffalo, antelopes, and abundant birdlife. Explore the floodplains and riverine forests, either on foot or by boat, and immerse yourself in the sights and sounds of the untamed wilderness.

Mozambique's wildlife and nature reserves offer a remarkable opportunity to witness the raw beauty of the natural world. Whether you choose to embark on a thrilling safari, dive into the vibrant underwater ecosystems, or simply relax on a secluded beach, the country's protected areas will leave you with memories to last a lifetime. Remember to respect the wildlife and the delicate balance of the ecosystems, and embrace the chance to connect with nature in its purest form.

CHAPTER 7

DIVING AND SNORKELING IN MOZAMBIQUE'S MARINE PARKS

Mozambique is a paradise for water enthusiasts, offering an abundance of marine life, pristine coral reefs, and crystal-clear waters. In this chapter, we will explore the magnificent world that lies beneath the surface as we delve into the captivating experiences of diving and snorkeling in Mozambique's marine parks. Whether you're a seasoned diver or a novice snorkeler, Mozambique's underwater treasures are sure to leave you awe-inspired.

Exploring the Marine Parks

Mozambique is home to several marine parks that have been established to protect the country's diverse marine ecosystems. The most renowned marine parks include the Bazaruto Archipelago National Park, the Quirimbas Archipelago National Park, and the Ponta do Ouro Partial Marine Reserve. These parks offer a haven for marine species and provide visitors with exceptional diving and snorkeling opportunities.

1. **Bazaruto Archipelago National Park**: Located off the coast of Vilanculos, the Bazaruto Archipelago

National Park is a tropical paradise renowned for its vibrant coral reefs, pristine beaches, and abundant marine life. Divers and snorkelers can explore a kaleidoscope of colorful corals, swim alongside graceful manta rays and whale sharks, and encounter a variety of tropical fish species. The park's protected status ensures that its underwater ecosystems remain intact, offering an unforgettable experience for nature enthusiasts.

2. **Quirimbas Archipelago National Park**: Situated in northern Mozambique, the Quirimbas Archipelago National Park is a hidden gem waiting to be discovered. With its secluded islands, turquoise waters, and extensive coral reefs, this park is a haven for underwater exploration. Diving and snorkeling in the Quirimbas Archipelago offer encounters with playful dolphins, sea turtles, and an array of vibrant coral gardens. The park's remote location ensures an untouched and pristine marine environment.

3. **Ponta do Ouro Partial Marine Reserve**: Located in southern Mozambique, the Ponta do Ouro Partial Marine Reserve is a popular destination for diving and snorkeling enthusiasts. Its proximity to the South African border makes it easily accessible for visitors

from nearby countries. The reserve is known for its diverse marine life, including dolphins, humpback whales, and elusive dugongs. The warm Indian Ocean waters teem with colorful fish species, making it a delight for snorkelers to explore the vibrant reefs.

Dive Sites and Snorkeling Spots

Mozambique offers a plethora of dive sites and snorkeling spots that cater to all levels of experience. From shallow reefs suitable for beginners to exhilarating deep-sea dives for advanced divers, there is something for everyone. Popular dive sites include Two-Mile Reef in Bazaruto, Neptune's Arm in Quirimbas, and Pinnacles in Ponta do Ouro. Snorkelers can enjoy the stunning coral gardens close to the shoreline, observing the incredible biodiversity just beneath the surface.

Marine Encounters

One of the highlights of diving and snorkeling in Mozambique is the opportunity to encounter magnificent marine creatures up close. Manta rays, whale sharks, dolphins, and turtles are among the charismatic species that you may encounter during your underwater adventures. The chance to witness these majestic creatures in their natural habitat is a truly humbling experience that leaves a lasting impression on visitors.

Dive Operators and Snorkeling Excursions

To make the most of your diving and snorkeling experiences, it is recommended to engage the services of reputable dive operators. These operators offer guided trips to the best dive sites and provide equipment, ensuring a safe and enjoyable experience. Snorkeling excursions are also available for those who prefer to stay close to the surface. Expert guides accompany snorkelers, pointing out the wonders of the underwater world and ensuring their safety.

Conservation and Responsible Diving

Mozambique's marine parks are committed to conservation efforts and sustainable tourism practices. As a responsible diver or snorkeler, it is essential to respect the fragile marine ecosystems, follow guidelines set by the marine parks, and avoid damaging corals or disturbing marine life. By adopting responsible diving practices, you contribute to the preservation of these invaluable natural resources for future generations.

Diving and snorkeling in Mozambique's marine parks offer a gateway to a world of awe-inspiring beauty and biodiversity. From the vibrant coral reefs to encounters with majestic marine creatures, Mozambique provides a truly unforgettable underwater experience. Whether you're exploring the Bazaruto Archipelago, the Quirimbas Archipelago, or the Ponta do Ouro Reserve, the marine parks of Mozambique are waiting to be explored, promising adventure, wonder, and a deep appreciation for the wonders of the ocean.

CHAPTER 8

UNVEILING MOZAMBIQUE'S ARCHITECTURAL HERITAGE

Mozambique's architectural heritage is a testament to the country's rich history and diverse cultural influences. From ancient ruins to colonial-era buildings, Mozambique's architecture tells the story of its past and present. In this chapter, we will embark on a journey to explore the architectural wonders that grace the landscapes of this fascinating nation.

Ancient Architecture

The history of Mozambique's architecture dates back centuries, with evidence of ancient civilizations leaving their mark on the land. One notable example is the Great Zimbabwe ruins, located in the southeastern part of the country. These impressive stone structures, built between the 11th and 15th centuries, provide a glimpse into the architectural prowess of the Shona people who once inhabited the region.

Another remarkable site is the Island of Mozambique, a UNESCO World Heritage site. This island served as the capital of Portuguese East Africa and showcases a blend of European, Arab, and African architectural styles.

The stone buildings, fortresses, and churches on the island stand as a testament to its historical significance.

Portuguese Colonial Architecture

During the era of Portuguese colonization, Mozambique experienced significant architectural development. The influence of Portuguese design and construction can be seen in many cities and towns across the country. One prime example is the city of Maputo, the capital of Mozambique. Here, you'll find an array of elegant colonial buildings that reflect the grandeur of the past. The Railway Station, built in the early 20th century, is an iconic landmark adorned with beautiful wrought-iron decorations and stunning architectural details.

Swahili Architecture

Along Mozambique's coastline, particularly in areas with Swahili heritage, you'll encounter a unique style of architecture that blends African, Arab, and Persian influences. Stone townhouses with ornate wooden doors and intricately carved balconies are characteristic of this architectural style.

Quelimane, a city with a strong Swahili heritage, offers a glimpse into this rich architectural tradition.

Modern Architecture

In recent years, Mozambique has witnessed a surge in modern architectural development, especially in urban centers. Maputo, in particular, showcases contemporary architectural marvels that stand alongside its historic buildings. The Samora Machel Statue, a towering monument honoring Mozambique's first president, is a striking example of modern sculpture and architecture.

Vernacular Architecture

In rural areas, Mozambique's vernacular architecture reflects the country's diverse ethnic groups and their traditional building techniques. Mud huts with thatched roofs, known as "chapas," can be found in villages across the country. These structures showcase the resourcefulness and adaptability of local communities, utilizing locally available materials to create sustainable and functional dwellings.

Conservation and Preservation Efforts

Preserving Mozambique's architectural heritage is of utmost importance.

Several organizations and initiatives are working tirelessly to restore and protect significant buildings and sites. Efforts are being made to promote sustainable tourism that contributes to the conservation of these architectural treasures.

Mozambique's architectural heritage is a tapestry woven with threads from ancient civilizations, colonial powers, and indigenous traditions. From the grandeur of Portuguese colonial buildings to the intricate details of Swahili architecture, Mozambique's diverse architectural styles offer a captivating glimpse into its past.

As you explore the architectural wonders of Mozambique, take a moment to appreciate the craftsmanship and cultural significance behind each structure. Whether you find yourself standing before ancient ruins, strolling through the streets of Maputo, or immersing yourself in the charm of rural villages, Mozambique's architectural heritage will leave an indelible impression on your journey through this captivating country.

CHAPTER 9

CUISINE AND CULINARY DELIGHTS OF MOZAMBIQUE

Mozambique is a country that tantalizes the taste buds with its vibrant and flavorful cuisine. Influenced by its rich history and diverse cultural heritage, Mozambican dishes offer a unique fusion of African, Portuguese, and Arab flavors. In this chapter, we will embark on a culinary journey through Mozambique, exploring its traditional dishes, fresh seafood, aromatic spices, and refreshing beverages.

Mozambican Flavors and Ingredients

Mozambican cuisine is characterized by the use of fresh and locally sourced ingredients, making the most of the country's abundant seafood, tropical fruits, vegetables, and aromatic spices. The cuisine reflects the coastal nature of the country, with an emphasis on fish, prawns, crabs, and other delectable seafood.

Piri Piri: The Fiery Spice

One cannot discuss Mozambican cuisine without mentioning piri piri, a spicy chili pepper that adds a fiery kick to many dishes. Piri piri is used to marinate meat, seafood, and vegetables, infusing them with a delicious heat. The unique blend of flavors in Mozambican cuisine is incomplete without the presence of piri piri.

Matapa: A Traditional Delicacy

One of Mozambique's most renowned traditional dishes is matapa, made from stewed cassava leaves, ground peanuts, coconut milk, garlic, and spices. This creamy and aromatic dish is often served with xima, a staple made from maize flour. Matapa is a testament to Mozambique's cultural diversity and its ability to transform simple ingredients into a complex and satisfying dish.

Prawns and Peri-Peri Chicken

Mozambique's coastline provides an abundance of fresh seafood, and prawns take center stage in many dishes. Grilled prawns marinated in piri piri sauce are a popular delicacy, offering a delightful combination of smoky flavors and a spicy kick. Peri-peri chicken, marinated in a fiery blend of spices and grilled to perfection, is another must-try dish that showcases Mozambique's love for bold flavors.

Cashew Nuts: A Mozambican Delight

Mozambique is one of the largest producers of cashew nuts in the world, and they play a significant role in the country's cuisine. Cashews are used in a variety of dishes, from savory stews to sweet desserts. One popular dish is cashew nut curry, where the creaminess of the nuts complements the spiciness of the curry sauce.

Zambezia Province: Home of the Zambezi Beer

Zambezia Province, located in central Mozambique, is known for its locally brewed Zambezi beer. This refreshing and crisp lager is made from locally grown barley and has become a popular choice among locals and visitors alike. Sampling Zambezi beer is not only a treat for the taste buds but also a way to connect with Mozambique's vibrant beer culture.

Tropical Fruits and Sweet Delights

Mozambique's tropical climate provides an abundance of mouthwatering fruits, including mangoes, pineapples, papayas, and bananas. These fruits are often enjoyed fresh, as a refreshing snack or as a complement to savory dishes. Additionally, Mozambique is famous for its coconut-based desserts, such as coconut rice pudding and coconut candies, offering a delightful end to a flavorful meal.

Mozambican Street Food

Exploring the vibrant street food scene in Mozambique is a must for any food lover. Street vendors offer an array of delectable snacks, from savory samosas and grilled skewers to fried cassava chips and spicy fritters. Indulging in street food allows you to experience the authentic flavors of Mozambique and engage with the local culinary traditions.

Traditional Mozambican Restaurants

For those seeking a more formal dining experience, Mozambique is home to numerous restaurants that specialize in traditional cuisine. These establishments showcase the country's culinary heritage through their diverse menus, warm hospitality, and charming ambience. Enjoying a meal at a traditional Mozambican restaurant offers a deeper understanding of the country's food culture and allows you to savor the complexity of flavors.

Fusion Cuisine and International Influences

As Mozambique continues to evolve, its cuisine has embraced various international influences, resulting in a fusion of flavors and culinary techniques. Fusion restaurants can be found in major cities, offering innovative dishes that blend Mozambican ingredients with global culinary trends. This culinary fusion represents Mozambique's openness to experimentation and its desire to create unique dining experiences.

Mozambican cuisine is a true reflection of the country's cultural diversity, natural abundance, and vibrant history. From the fiery heat of piri piri to the delicate flavors of freshly caught seafood, each dish tells a story and invites you to savor the essence of Mozambique. Whether you're exploring street food stalls, indulging in traditional restaurants, or discovering hidden culinary gems, the cuisine of Mozambique will leave a lasting impression on your palate. So, prepare your taste buds for an unforgettable gastronomic adventure as you immerse yourself in the captivating flavors of Mozambique.

CHAPTER 10

ADVENTURE ACTIVITIES: FROM SAFARIS TO WATER SPORTS

Mozambique is a land of thrilling adventures, where nature's wonders and adrenaline-pumping activities come together. From exhilarating safaris to exciting water sports, this chapter will take you on a journey through the heart-pounding experiences that await you in this captivating country.

Safari Expeditions

Mozambique is home to several national parks and wildlife reserves, offering incredible opportunities for unforgettable safari adventures. One such gem is Gorongosa National Park, known for its diverse ecosystems and abundant wildlife. Embark on a game drive through the park, accompanied by experienced guides who will lead you to encounters with majestic elephants, graceful antelopes, and the elusive predators that roam these lands.

Canoeing and Kayaking

For a unique and serene adventure, explore Mozambique's rivers and mangroves by canoe or kayak.

Glide along the Zambezi River, where you can witness the breathtaking beauty of the surrounding landscapes and observe a rich variety of bird species. Paddle through the tranquil channels of the Bazaruto Archipelago, immersing yourself in the pristine coastal scenery and encountering marine life along the way.

Horseback Riding

Saddle up for an exhilarating horseback ride along the stunning beaches of Mozambique. Feel the wind in your hair as you gallop through the waves, creating an unforgettable connection with these magnificent creatures. Whether you are an experienced rider or a beginner, there are options available for all levels of equestrian enthusiasts.

Dhow Cruises

Experience the traditional charm of Mozambique by embarking on a dhow cruise. These elegant wooden sailing boats have been used for centuries along the East African coast and provide a unique way to explore Mozambique's islands and coastline. Relax on board as you sail into the sunset, savoring delicious seafood and enjoying the gentle sway of the waves.

Scuba Diving and Snorkeling

Mozambique is a paradise for underwater enthusiasts, with its crystal-clear waters and vibrant coral reefs. Dive into a world of colorful marine life, encountering tropical fish, graceful manta rays, and even the magnificent whale sharks. Whether you are a certified diver or a beginner, there are dive centers and snorkeling spots that cater to all skill levels, ensuring an awe-inspiring experience beneath the waves.

Deep-Sea Fishing

Reel in the adventure with deep-sea fishing in Mozambique's bountiful waters. Known for its exceptional game fishing, Mozambique offers the chance to catch trophy-sized fish such as marlin, sailfish, and barracuda. Charter a fishing boat and embark on an exciting expedition, guided by experienced captains who know the best spots to find these prized catches.

Quad Biking

Embark on an adrenaline-fueled quad biking excursion through Mozambique's stunning landscapes. Ride through sandy dunes, lush forests, and rural villages, immersing yourself in the country's natural beauty.

Whether you prefer a thrilling off-road adventure or a leisurely ride along the coastline, quad biking provides a unique perspective and a thrilling way to explore Mozambique's diverse terrain.

Paragliding and Skydiving

For the ultimate thrill-seekers, Mozambique offers the opportunity to soar high above its breathtaking landscapes. Take to the skies with paragliding, experiencing the exhilaration of flying while taking in panoramic views of the coastline. For the most daring adventurers, skydiving provides an unmatched adrenaline rush as you freefall through the sky before landing on the sandy shores below.

Rock Climbing and Abseiling

Challenge yourself mentally and physically with rock climbing and abseiling adventures in Mozambique's stunning mountainous regions. Climb towering cliffs, conquer challenging routes, and enjoy breathtaking vistas from the top. With a variety of climbing sites suitable for different skill levels, Mozambique welcomes climbers of all abilities to test their limits.

Wildlife Tracking and Conservation

Immerse yourself in the world of wildlife tracking and conservation by participating in conservation programs in Mozambique. Join expert guides and researchers to monitor and protect endangered species such as lions, elephants, and rhinos. Contribute to the preservation of Mozambique's rich biodiversity while gaining a deeper understanding of the challenges and efforts involved in wildlife conservation.

From the heart-stopping encounters of a safari to the exhilarating water sports and outdoor activities, Mozambique offers a wide array of adventure opportunities for every thrill-seeker. Prepare to push your boundaries, experience the raw beauty of nature, and create memories that will last a lifetime. Let Mozambique be your playground of adventure, where excitement and exploration await at every turn.

CHAPTER 11

EXPLORING MOZAMBIQUE'S ART AND HANDICRAFTS

In the diverse cultural tapestry of Mozambique, art and handicrafts play a significant role in expressing the country's history, traditions, and creative spirit. From intricate wood carvings to vibrant textiles, Mozambique offers a treasure trove of artistic expressions that reflect the country's rich heritage and the ingenuity of its people. In this chapter, we embark on a journey to explore the world of Mozambican art and handicrafts, delving into the techniques, symbolism, and cultural significance behind these unique creations.

Traditional Crafts

Mozambique's traditional crafts showcase the creativity and skill of its artisans. Wood carving holds a special place in Mozambican craftsmanship, with intricate sculptures that depict human figures, animals, and mythological creatures. These carvings often have spiritual or ceremonial significance, portraying ancestral spirits or serving as objects of worship. The Makonde people, renowned for their exceptional wood carving skills, create exquisite pieces that are highly sought after by collectors and art enthusiasts.

Basketry is another traditional craft deeply rooted in Mozambique's cultural heritage. Local communities skillfully weave baskets using natural fibers such as palm leaves and sisal. These baskets serve both functional and decorative purposes, ranging from storage containers to intricate designs that incorporate geometric patterns and vibrant colors. The craftsmanship behind these baskets is a testament to the dexterity and artistry of Mozambique's artisans.

Contemporary Art

While traditional crafts hold a significant place in Mozambique's artistic landscape, contemporary art is also thriving in the country. The post-independence era marked a turning point for Mozambican art, as artists began to use their work as a means of social and political commentary. From paintings and sculptures to mixed media installations, contemporary Mozambican art reflects the country's history, struggles, and aspirations.

Renowned artists like Malangatana Ngwenya and Bertina Lopes have gained international recognition for their thought-provoking and visually captivating creations. Malangatana's paintings often depict scenes from Mozambique's turbulent past, exploring themes of colonialism, war, and liberation. Bertina Lopes, on the other hand, uses her art to celebrate

Mozambican women and their resilience, employing bold colors and expressive brushstrokes.

Textiles and Embroidery

Mozambique's textile traditions are as diverse as its cultural heritage. The country is known for its vibrant fabrics, often adorned with intricate embroidery and beadwork. Traditional garments such as capulana, a colorful sarong-like cloth, are an integral part of Mozambique's identity. Each region of the country has its distinctive textile patterns and motifs, representing the local customs and beliefs.

The art of embroidery is particularly cherished in Mozambique, with skilled artisans creating intricate designs on clothing, household items, and ceremonial regalia. These embroideries often tell stories and carry symbolic meaning, conveying messages of love, fertility, or protection. Mozambican embroidery is characterized by its meticulous attention to detail and the use of vibrant threads that bring the designs to life.

Artistic Influences

Mozambican art has been shaped by various cultural influences over the centuries. The country's proximity to the Swahili Coast and its historical connections with Arab traders have infused elements of Islamic art into Mozambican craftsmanship. Intricate geometric patterns, calligraphy, and arabesque motifs can be seen in wood carvings, architecture, and pottery.

Furthermore, Mozambique's colonial past under Portuguese rule has left its mark on the country's art scene. European artistic traditions and techniques have influenced Mozambican artists, leading to a fusion of styles and artistic expressions. This blending of influences has given rise to a unique and diverse art landscape that reflects Mozambique's multicultural identity.

Exploring Mozambique's art and handicrafts is a captivating journey into the heart of the country's cultural heritage. From the traditional craftsmanship that has been passed down through generations to the contemporary art scene that challenges social norms, Mozambique offers a vibrant tapestry of creativity and expression.

Whether you appreciate the intricate wood carvings, the vibrant textiles, or the thought-provoking contemporary artworks, immersing yourself in Mozambique's art world is an opportunity to connect with the country's soul and its people. So, take the time to visit local artisans, explore art galleries, and witness the beauty that lies within Mozambique's artistic endeavors.

CHAPTER 12

FESTIVALS AND CULTURAL EVENTS IN MOZAMBIQUE

Mozambique is a country rich in cultural diversity, and one of the best ways to experience this vibrant tapestry is by attending its festivals and cultural events. Throughout the year, Mozambicans come together to celebrate their heritage, traditions, and customs, creating a lively atmosphere filled with music, dance, food, and community spirit. In this chapter, we will explore some of the most captivating festivals and cultural events that take place in different regions of Mozambique.

Marrabenta Festival

One of the most popular music festivals in Mozambique is the Marrabenta Festival. Celebrated in Maputo, the capital city, this event showcases the country's traditional music genre known as Marrabenta. Originating in the 1930s, Marrabenta combines Portuguese and African influences, resulting in a lively and rhythmic sound. During the festival, local musicians and bands take the stage, captivating the audience with their energetic performances.

Visitors can also participate in dance workshops to learn the traditional moves associated with Marrabenta.

Festival de Canhoto

In the northern province of Nampula, the Festival de Canhoto is a unique celebration of Mozambique's oral traditions. Canhoto, a form of oral poetry, is recited by skilled poets who captivate the audience with their storytelling abilities. The festival gathers renowned Canhoto poets from across the country, providing a platform for them to showcase their talent and keep this traditional art form alive. It's a mesmerizing experience to witness the power of words as the poets narrate tales of love, history, and everyday life in Mozambique.

Chopi Music and Dance Festival

In the Inhambane Province, the Chopi Music and Dance Festival offers a glimpse into the rich cultural heritage of the Chopi people. This festival celebrates the unique music and dance styles of the Chopi community, characterized by intricate melodies, polyrhythmic beats, and mesmerizing choreography. Visitors can enjoy performances by traditional orchestras playing xylophones, marimbas, and drums, accompanied by graceful dancers adorned in vibrant costumes.

The festival provides a wonderful opportunity to immerse oneself in the rhythms and movements of Chopi culture.

Festival de Lhanguene

The Festival de Lhanguene, held in the central city of Beira, showcases the vibrant traditions of the Ndau people. This festival is a colorful display of Ndau music, dance, and craftsmanship. The highlight of the event is the Lhanguene procession, where participants dress in traditional attire, adorned with elaborate beadwork and feathers, while singing and dancing through the streets. The festival also features exhibitions of Ndau art, including intricate woodcarvings, woven baskets, and pottery. It's a fantastic opportunity to witness the artistic expressions and cultural pride of the Ndau community.

Mozambique Fashion Week

For fashion enthusiasts, the Mozambique Fashion Week held in Maputo is a must-attend event. This glamorous affair brings together local and international designers to showcase their collections inspired by Mozambican culture and trends.

From traditional designs fused with contemporary styles to avant-garde creations, the Mozambique Fashion Week highlights the creativity and talent of Mozambican fashion industry. The runway shows, exhibitions, and workshops create a platform for emerging designers to gain recognition and contribute to the growth of the country's fashion scene.

Festival of the Islands

As an archipelago, Mozambique's islands have a unique cultural identity, and the Festival of the Islands celebrates their heritage. This annual event takes place in the stunning Bazaruto Archipelago and attracts locals and tourists alike. The festival features traditional music and dance performances, showcasing the diverse cultural influences that have shaped the island communities. Visitors can also indulge in delicious seafood delicacies, participate in water sports activities, and explore the natural beauty of the islands. The Festival of the Islands is a perfect blend of cultural immersion and island paradise experience.

Mapiko Mask Festival

In the northern region of Mozambique, the Makonde people celebrate their culture through the Mapiko Mask Festival. The festival centers around the Mapiko masks, which are intricately carved wooden masks representing ancestral spirits. During the festival, dancers wearing the masks perform intricate choreographies, accompanied by the rhythmic sounds of drums and other traditional instruments. The masked dancers often engage in storytelling, conveying moral lessons and historical narratives. The Mapiko Mask Festival offers a captivating glimpse into the spiritual beliefs and cultural heritage of the Makonde people.

Independence Day Celebrations

On June 25th, Mozambique commemorates its independence from Portuguese colonial rule. The Independence Day celebrations take place across the country, with the largest festivities held in Maputo. The day begins with a military parade, showcasing Mozambique's defense forces and their achievements. The streets come alive with colorful processions, music, and dance performances, reflecting the patriotic spirit of the Mozambican people. The celebrations also include speeches, fireworks displays, and cultural events that highlight the country's progress and unity since gaining independence.

These are just a few examples of the diverse festivals and cultural events that take place throughout Mozambique.

Attending these celebrations provides a unique opportunity to immerse oneself in the country's rich heritage, interact with locals, and create unforgettable memories. Whether it's the rhythmic beats of Marrabenta, the mesmerizing performances of traditional dancers, or the artistic expressions found in craftsmanship and fashion, Mozambique's festivals offer a captivating journey into the heart and soul of the nation.

CHAPTER 13

UNCOVERING HIDDEN GEMS IN MOZAMBIQUE

As you embark on your journey through Mozambique, it's time to go off the beaten path and discover the country's hidden gems. While popular tourist destinations offer their own allure, it is in the lesser-known corners of Mozambique that you'll find true treasures waiting to be explored. In this chapter, we will guide you through a selection of these hidden gems, unveiling the beauty, tranquility, and cultural richness that lie off the tourist radar.

Quirimbas Archipelago

Tucked away in the northern reaches of Mozambique, the Quirimbas Archipelago is a collection of 32 islands surrounded by turquoise waters. From the pristine beaches of Ibo Island to the remote wilderness of Quirimba Island, this archipelago offers a haven for nature lovers and adventure seekers alike. Immerse yourself in the rich marine life as you snorkel or dive along vibrant coral reefs, or delve into the archipelago's history by exploring the ancient fortresses and trading posts.

Niassa Reserve

For those seeking a true wilderness experience, Niassa Reserve is a hidden gem in the northern part of Mozambique. Covering an astounding 42,000 square kilometers (16,200 square miles), this reserve is one of the largest protected areas in Africa. Its diverse landscapes encompass miombo woodlands, riverine forests, and grassy plains, providing a haven for an abundance of wildlife. Embark on a thrilling safari adventure and encounter elephants, lions, zebras, and the elusive African wild dog.

Ilha de Mozambique

Step back in time as you visit Ilha de Mozambique, a UNESCO World Heritage site and an island steeped in history. This small island, located off the northern coast, was once the capital of Portuguese East Africa. Explore the cobbled streets lined with colonial-era buildings, visit the imposing Fortress of São Sebastião, and immerse yourself in the island's vibrant mix of African, Arab, and European cultures. The island's rich heritage and architectural beauty make it a must-visit destination for history enthusiasts.

Chimanimani Mountains

Nestled on Mozambique's eastern border with Zimbabwe, the Chimanimani Mountains offer a haven for hikers and nature lovers. With their jagged peaks, cascading waterfalls, and lush forests, these mountains provide breathtaking scenery and abundant wildlife. Embark on a trekking expedition and conquer towering peaks, encounter unique bird species, and relish the serenity of nature as you camp under starlit skies.

Lake Niassa

Discover the hidden jewel of Lake Niassa, also known as Lake Malawi, which stretches across Mozambique's western border. This vast freshwater lake is teeming with life, hosting an array of colorful fish species found nowhere else in the world. Dive into the crystal-clear waters and snorkel alongside the endemic cichlids, or simply relax on the lakeshore, surrounded by tranquility and untouched beauty.

Tete

Venture inland to the city of Tete, located on the banks of the Zambezi River. While Tete is known for its coal mines and trade routes, it also offers historical sites and cultural encounters.

Visit the famous Swahili-style Tete Cathedral, dating back to the 16th century, and explore the local markets where you can immerse yourself in the vibrant atmosphere and sample traditional Mozambican cuisine.

Bazaruto Archipelago

Escape to the pristine paradise of the Bazaruto Archipelago, a collection of islands off the southern coast of Mozambique. With its turquoise waters, powdery white sand beaches, and thriving marine life, this archipelago is a haven for beach enthusiasts and marine adventurers. Dive into the azure depths to witness the majestic dugongs, swim with dolphins, and marvel at the vibrant coral reefs.

Gorongosa National Park

Journey to Gorongosa National Park, situated in the heart of Mozambique. Once devastated by civil unrest, this park has made a remarkable recovery and is now a symbol of conservation success. Explore the park's diverse ecosystems, from floodplains to savannahs, and witness the incredible resurgence of wildlife. Join a guided safari and spot elephants, lions, hippos, and a myriad of bird species as they thrive in this protected sanctuary.

Inhaca Island

Located just a short boat ride from Maputo, Inhaca Island is a tranquil oasis offering sandy beaches, crystal-clear waters, and abundant marine life. Take a break from the mainland and unwind on the idyllic shores, go snorkeling to discover the vibrant coral reefs, or explore the island's mangrove forests teeming with fascinating bird species. For a truly unique experience, visit the Marine Biology Museum and witness sea turtle hatchlings being released into the ocean.

Mount Namuli

For adventurous souls and avid mountaineers, Mount Namuli beckons in the northern part of Mozambique. Rising to a height of 2,419 meters (7,936 feet), this majestic peak offers a thrilling challenge and rewards climbers with panoramic views of the surrounding landscape. As you ascend, marvel at the diverse flora and fauna that call this mountain home and bask in the sense of accomplishment when you reach the summit.

These hidden gems of Mozambique are just a glimpse into the country's vast array of off-the-beaten-path treasures. From pristine islands to unexplored wilderness, each destination holds its own unique charm, ready to captivate and inspire adventurous travelers. As you venture beyond the well-trodden routes, you'll discover a Mozambique that few have experienced, a Mozambique that will leave an indelible mark on your heart and soul. So, pack your curiosity, embrace the unknown, and let Mozambique's hidden gems unveil their secrets to you.

CHAPTER 14

SUSTAINABLE TOURISM IN MOZAMBIQUE: RESPONSIBLE TRAVEL PRACTICES

As travelers, we have a responsibility to preserve the beauty and cultural heritage of the places we visit. In Mozambique, a country blessed with diverse ecosystems and rich cultural traditions, sustainable tourism practices are vital for the long-term well-being of both the environment and local communities. In this chapter, we will explore the concept of sustainable tourism and provide practical tips on how to be a responsible traveler in Mozambique.

Understanding Sustainable Tourism

Sustainable tourism aims to minimize the negative impacts of travel on the environment, while maximizing the positive social and economic benefits for local communities. It is about finding a balance between enjoying the natural and cultural wonders of a destination and ensuring their preservation for future generations.

Preserving Mozambique's Natural Environment

Mozambique is home to an incredible array of natural wonders, including pristine beaches, coral reefs, mangroves, and national parks. To help preserve these fragile ecosystems, consider the following tips:

1. Respect Marine Life: When snorkeling or diving, avoid touching or damaging coral reefs and refrain from disturbing marine life. Use reef-safe sunscreen to minimize chemical pollution.

2. Reduce Plastic Waste: Carry a reusable water bottle and say no to single-use plastics. Dispose of your waste responsibly and participate in beach clean-up initiatives if available.

3. Conserve Water: Be mindful of water usage, especially in regions where water scarcity is a concern. Take shorter showers and report any leaks or wastage to your accommodation provider.

4. Support Conservation Efforts: Consider visiting marine protected areas and national parks that actively contribute to the preservation of Mozambique's biodiversity. Your entrance fees often support conservation initiatives.

Cultural Respect and Empowerment

Mozambique's cultural heritage is a tapestry woven with diverse ethnic groups, traditions, and languages. To engage respectfully with local communities and contribute positively to their well-being:

1. Learn Basic Phrases: Take the time to learn a few basic phrases in the local language, such as greetings and thank-yous. This effort shows respect for the local culture and fosters meaningful connections.

2. Dress Appropriately: Respect cultural norms by dressing modestly, particularly when visiting religious sites or rural communities. Research local customs and traditions to ensure your attire aligns with local expectations.

3. Support Local Businesses: Seek out locally owned accommodations, restaurants, and tour operators. By supporting local enterprises, you contribute directly to the economic empowerment of the community.

4. Engage in Responsible Souvenir Shopping: Avoid purchasing products made from endangered species, such as ivory or turtle shells. Instead, opt for locally crafted souvenirs that support local artisans and promote sustainable livelihoods.

Responsible Wildlife Encounters

Mozambique's national parks offer incredible opportunities to witness diverse wildlife, including elephants, lions, and rare bird species. To ensure your wildlife encounters are ethical and sustainable:

1. Choose Responsible Tour Operators: Select tour operators that prioritize ethical wildlife practices, such as maintaining a safe distance from animals and following responsible safari driving guidelines.

2. Say No to Animal Exploitation: Avoid participating in activities that involve riding elephants, visiting captive animal shows, or supporting establishments that exploit wildlife for entertainment purposes.

3. Follow Park Rules and Regulations: Respect park rules, including designated trails, speed limits, and restrictions on feeding or approaching wildlife. These guidelines are in place to protect both animals and visitors.

4. Support Conservation Projects: Consider donating to local conservation organizations or volunteering for wildlife monitoring and research programs. Your contribution can make a significant impact on wildlife protection efforts.

Sustainable tourism is the key to preserving Mozambique's natural wonders, protecting its cultural heritage, and uplifting local communities. By embracing responsible travel practices, you can leave a positive footprint on the places you visit and ensure that future generations can continue to enjoy the beauty and diversity of Mozambique. Remember, every small action counts, and together, we can make a difference in creating a sustainable and vibrant future for Mozambique's tourism industry.

CHAPTER 15

PRACTICAL INFORMATION AND TRAVEL TIPS

As you embark on your journey to Mozambique, it's essential to be well-prepared with practical information and travel tips. This chapter will provide you with valuable insights to ensure a smooth and enjoyable experience throughout your trip. From visa requirements to health and safety tips, let's dive into the essential details you need to know before setting foot in this captivating country.

1. **Visa Requirements**: Before traveling to Mozambique, it's crucial to understand the visa requirements. Most visitors will need a visa to enter the country, which can be obtained in advance from Mozambican embassies or consulates in your home country. Alternatively, some nationalities can obtain a visa on arrival at major entry points such as airports and border crossings. However, it's recommended to check the latest visa regulations and requirements prior to your trip, as they may vary based on your nationality.

2. **Currency and Money Matters**: The official currency of Mozambique is the Mozambican Metical (MZN).

While some establishments may accept major foreign currencies such as the US Dollar and the Euro, it's advisable to have local currency for day-to-day transactions. ATMs are available in major cities and tourist areas, where you can withdraw cash using your debit or credit card. However, it's always a good idea to carry some cash in smaller denominations for places where card payments may not be accepted. Be sure to notify your bank about your travel plans to avoid any issues with card transactions.

3. **Language**: The official language of Mozambique is Portuguese, a legacy of its colonial past. While Portuguese is widely spoken, especially in urban areas, English is also understood and spoken in many tourist destinations, hotels, and restaurants. However, it's useful to learn a few basic Portuguese phrases, as it will enhance your interactions with locals and showcase your appreciation for the local culture.

4. **Health and Safety**: Ensuring your health and safety should be a top priority during your visit to Mozambique. Here are some important tips to keep in mind:

- Vaccinations: Check with your healthcare provider or travel clinic for recommended vaccinations before traveling to Mozambique. Common vaccinations include those for hepatitis A and B, typhoid, tetanus, and yellow fever, depending on your medical history and the areas you plan to visit.

- Malaria: Mozambique is a malaria-endemic country, so it's essential to take necessary precautions. Consult with your healthcare professional about antimalarial medication and follow preventive measures such as using mosquito repellents, wearing long-sleeved clothing, and sleeping under mosquito nets, especially in high-risk areas.

- Water and Food Safety: To avoid waterborne diseases, it's advisable to drink bottled or boiled water. Additionally, be cautious when consuming food from street vendors and ensure that it's freshly prepared and cooked thoroughly.

- Travel Insurance: It's highly recommended to purchase travel insurance that covers medical emergencies, trip cancellation or interruption, and lost or stolen belongings. Review the policy details carefully to ensure it meets your specific needs.

- Personal Safety: Mozambique is generally a safe country for travelers, but it's important to take common-sense precautions. Avoid displaying valuable items openly, particularly in crowded places. Be aware of your surroundings, especially at night, and use reputable transportation options.

5. **Transportation**: Getting around Mozambique requires careful planning, as the infrastructure can vary in different regions. Here are some transportation options to consider:

- Domestic Flights: Mozambique has several domestic airports that connect major cities and popular tourist destinations. Domestic flights offer convenience and save time if you plan to cover long distances.

- Public Transport: Buses and minibusses, known as "chapas," are the most common form of public transportation in Mozambique. While they are affordable, they can be crowded and less comfortable for long journeys. It's advisable to check the schedules in advance and be prepared for potential delays.

- Car Rental: Renting a car provides flexibility and convenience, especially for exploring remote areas. However, it's essential to have a valid international driver's license, be familiar with local driving regulations, and ensure you have comprehensive insurance coverage.

- Taxis: Taxis are available in major cities and towns, and they are a convenient way to get around. Make sure to negotiate the fare in advance or insist on using a metered taxi to avoid any misunderstandings.

6. **Climate and What to Pack**: Mozambique has a tropical climate, with two distinct seasons: the dry season (from May to October) and the wet season (from November to April). The dry season is characterized by warm temperatures and lower humidity, while the wet season brings rainfall and higher humidity.

When packing for your trip, consider the following:

- Lightweight and breathable clothing: Pack light, loose-fitting clothing made from natural fibers to stay comfortable in the heat. Don't forget to include a hat, sunglasses, and sunscreen for sun protection.

- Rain gear: If you're traveling during the wet season, pack a lightweight rain jacket or poncho to stay dry during unexpected showers.

- Beach essentials: Mozambique's stunning beaches and islands are a highlight for many travelers. Don't forget to pack swimwear, beach towels, and reef-safe sunscreen for enjoyable beach days.

- Insect repellent: To protect yourself from mosquitoes and other insects, pack a reliable insect repellent containing DEET or another effective ingredient.

- Medications and first aid kit: Bring any necessary prescription medications, as well as a basic first aid kit with essentials like band-aids, antiseptic cream, and over-the-counter pain relievers.

7. **Cultural Etiquette**: Respecting the local culture and customs is important while traveling in Mozambique. Here are a few etiquette tips:

- Greetings: It's customary to greet people with a handshake, and it's polite to use the right hand for greetings and eating.

- Dress modestly: When visiting rural areas or religious sites, it's appropriate to dress modestly, covering your shoulders and knees as a sign of respect.

- Photography: Always ask for permission before taking photos of people, especially in more remote areas.

Some individuals may request a small fee for being photographed.

- Local customs: Embrace the local customs and traditions with an open mind. Learn about the cultural practices and customs of the communities you visit, and be respectful of their beliefs.

As you absorb the practical information and travel tips provided in this chapter, you'll be well-equipped to make the most of your Mozambique adventure. Remember to plan ahead, stay informed about any travel advisories, and embrace the warm hospitality and diverse experiences that this enchanting country has to offer. Bon voyage!

Printed in Great Britain
by Amazon

33603290R00050